Hopes, Dreams & Wishes

Hopes, Dreams & Wishes

A trilogy by
Nancy Vittorini, Joan Wilson, and Ellen Duris

♥

Illustrated and designed by
Ellen Duris

WINGS BOOKS
New York · Avenel, New Jersey

This 1994 edition is published by Wings Books,
distributed by Random House Value Publishing, Inc.,
40 Engelhard Avenue, Avenel, New Jersey 07001,
by arrangement with the authors.

Random House
New York · Toronto · London · Sydney · Auckland

Printed and bound in the United States of America

A CIP catalog record for this book
is available from the Library of Congress.

ISBN 0-517-11992-7

8 7 6 5 4 3 2 1

PART I

Hopes

Children hope birthdays will come twice a year.

Crafty magicians
hope rabbits appear.

Pilots hope breezes
lift airplane wings clear.

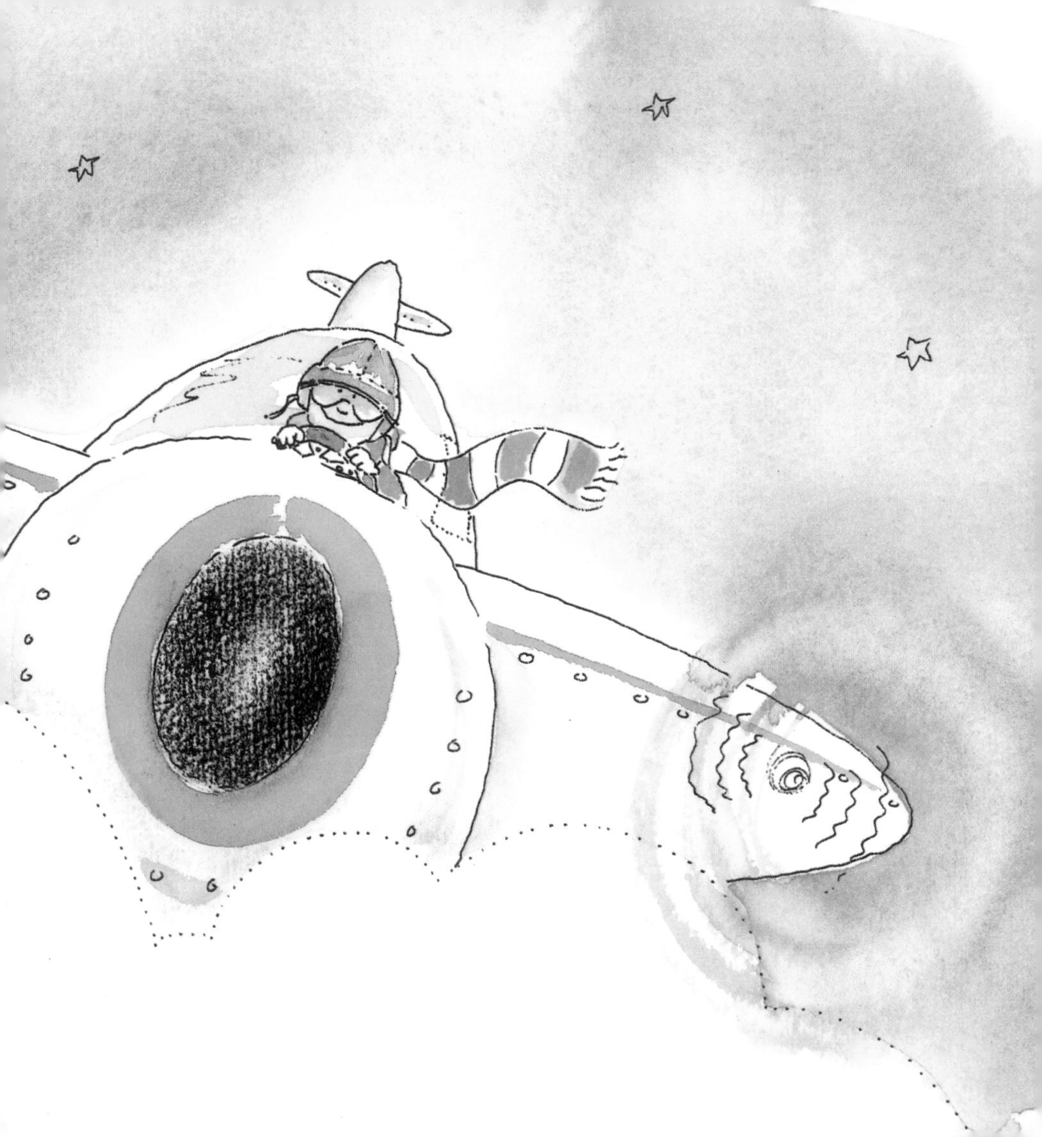

Country mouse hopes
he's a space pioneer.

Bird hopes to rest weary wings
way up here.

Trees hope for friends
like the bear, squirrel,
and deer.

"I will reach the top,"
hopes the brave mountaineer.

Mom hopes for smiles
through a bruise and a tear.

Secrets hope to be whispered
so soft in your ear.

Keep your hopes as high

as the roar of a cheer.

PART II

Dreams

Dogs dream of dinosaur bones cooked well-done.

Spiders dream
of delicate webs to be spun.

Some flowers dream
they can reach for the sun.

Rocking horse dreams
he can gallop and run.

Clowns dream of giggles
from grumpy-faced ones.

Buns dream of swirls
of sweet cinnamon.

Rollercoasters dream
of hair-raising fun.

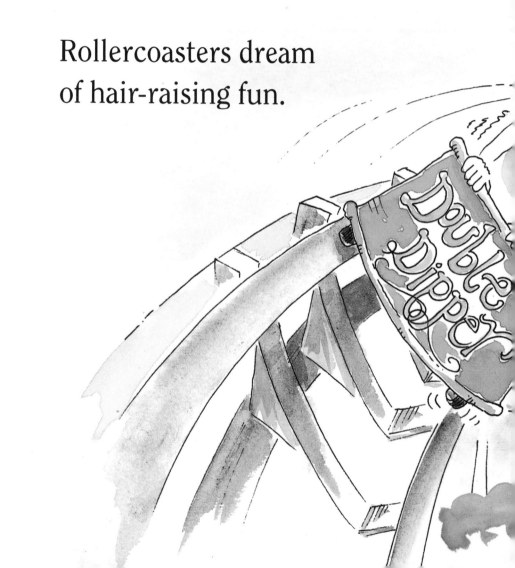

Elephants dream of peanuts by the ton!

Sneakers dream
Olympic games will be won.

When we dream big dreams,
our future's begun.

PART III

Wishes

Hot air balloons wish to float
with the breeze.

Tugboats wish bravely to sail seven seas.

Ice skaters wish
for smooth waters
that freeze.

Cats wish for fat mice to tickle and tease.

Crickets wish for nightfall
and musical knees.

Polar bears wish for
a warm, tender squeeze.

Dads wish for gardens
of sweet English peas.

Koalas wish for
a snooze in the trees.

Moms wish to hear the words "thank-you" and "please."

Your wish can come true;
the best come in three's.